T0130367

A Friendly Turtle and Five Dogs

Lulu the turtle,
Princess, Peanut, Fluffy, Scottie, and Snowman

Written and Designed by
Annie Lee

Copyright © 2016 by Annie Lee. 730425

ISBN: Softcover   978-1-5144-5044-4
        EBook   978-1-5144-5043-7

All rights reserved. No part of this book may be reproduced
or transmitted in any form or by any means, electronic
or mechanical, including photocopying, recording, or
by any information storage and retrieval system, without
permission in writing from the copyright owner.

Print information available on the last page

Rev. date: 07/18/2016

To order additional copies of this book, contact:
Xlibris
1-888-795-4274
www.Xlibris.com
Orders@Xlibris.com

Dedication

I dedicate this book to all of my nine grandchildren and two great grand-children. My grandchildren names from the oldest to the youngest. Erwin Cooper Jr, Sean J. Davis, Chrisheena L. Lee, LaNyia T. Kemp, Katauvis Manuel, Shakori Manuel, Nevaeh M. Joseph, Kayleigh McCoy-Lee and Neriah M. Wheeler. My great grandchildren are Lovely Jade Honeycutt-Cooper and Zavion Holloway-Davis. If there be any future grandchildren I also dedicate this book to them also. My God-children, Ja'Kayla L. Beauchamp and Daeshon D. Johnson I dedicate this book to them too.

Acknowledgements

I thank God for putting it on my heart to write this book. I acknowledge Miss Mary Cathy Malveaux for allowing me to write this book about her and her pets. I thank her for taking very good care of Lulu the turtle and the five dogs. They are a lot to deal with by themselves. I acknowledge my husband (Mr. Johnie) for allowing me to write about him and bringing the turtle home. I thank him for allowing Miss Cathy to take the turtle home and keep it. I thank Mrs. Iris Malveaux, who is Miss Cathy's sister for helping me write this story and giving me some good points about the story. I thank my family and all those that encouraged me to write another book.

Thank you, Thank you and Thank you!!!!

A Turtle Is Found

One day Mr. Johnie was cutting this yard. He saw a turtle and was surprised! There was a turtle in the grass in the back yard near the fence. He stopped cutting the yard and started looking for something to place the turtle in. He placed the turtle in an old milk crate until he finished cutting and trimming the yard.

After he finished the yard, he put the turtle on the back of the truck. The truck was secure because it had a tailgate on the back of the truck. He looked through the back window to see if the turtle was okay. The turtle had crawled through a hole in the old milk crate. It climbed up on the rim of the truck and was getting ready to fall off. Mr. Johnie slowed down and pulled over and then came to a stop. He put the turtle in the crate and closed the hole in the crate with an object until he got home.

The Turtle is Brought Home

Mr. Johnie brought the turtle to his house. He asked Miss Cathy, the neighbor, if she wanted the turtle. Miss Cathy lives across the street from his house. She said that she wanted to keep it. This was a large turtle not a little one. Miss Cathy took the turtle from Mr. Johnie and was not afraid. She used her bare hands and no gloves for protection. The turtle kept her head in the shell.

Miss Cathy loves animals and she keeps her five dogs healthy. The dogs' names are Scottie, Peanut, Princess, Snowman and Fluffy.

The Turtle Has A New Home

They saw the turtle and it was strange to them. The dogs were trying to smell the turtle. They knew that the turtle didn't smell like them. It did not bark at all. The turtle was very quiet. They watched Miss Cathy pick up the turtle and feed it. Miss Cathy named the turtle Lulu.

Lulu knew she was somewhere different. She did not move a lot for a couple of days. The surroundings around her were very strange. At first, the dogs wanted to play with her and she did not respond the way that they wanted her to. She did not run and jump like they did. Also the turtle did not have a bark.

Ms. Cathy and Lulu

Lulu is Hungry

Lulu did not like the lettuce that was given to her at first. She saw the dogs bowl with water and dog food. She would go and eat the dogs' food mixed with water. Lulu loved to eat fish and shrimp also. Miss Cathy would go to the stores and buy fresh fish and shrimp for Lulu. The turtle loved to eat her food in a big pot or tub with water in it.

Lulu loved to be in water in the back yard in the summer time. She would walk to the tub so that Ms. Cathy could put her in. Miss Cathy made Lulu a pond and put water in it.

Lulu Is Pampered

Maybe from the beginning the dogs were jealous of Lulu but, they got used to seeing the turtle around. The turtle got used to seeing her five friends also. The dogs still wanted to play with her all the time whenever they saw her.

Lulu loved Miss Cathy to pamper her. She fed her all the time when she thought that Lulu was hungry and thirsty. Lulu knew that that she was in a friendly place. The Lady of the house wanted to keep her alive and happy any way she could. She wanted Lulu to be comfortable. Miss Cathy had a new friend also.

Lulu's Five Friends

The first dog to the left is Peanut, on the other side of Ms. Cathy is Princess, Scottie is on the right side of Princess, Snowman is on the outside (she is white), and Fluffy is in the front of the driveway. These are Lulu the turtle friends.

Five Dogs Posing For This Picture

Miss Mary Cathy Malveaux also.

Mr. Johnie Hackett Jr.

Lulu is Hiding Out

One day Miss Cathy was looking for Lulu and she was hiding. She wondered; where could she be? Later on, that day she came out of the grass so that Miss Cathy could see her. Miss Cathy thought that Lulu was gone and that she would not see her anymore.

Lulu acted as though she was a pet turtle to someone else before Mr. Johnie found her. Lulu never tried to bite Miss Cathy or the dogs. She knew when it was time to eat or to move on. When it was time to get in the water, she went toward the water pond or large pot to get cool. She knew Miss Cathy would pick her up and put her in there.

Lulu comes in the House On Her Own

One day Lulu came in the house through the patio door. Lulu sometimes would come in the kitchen. Miss Cathy would leave the patio door open for the dogs to go out in the backyard and come in when they wanted to.

Lulu was a very special turtle to Miss Cathy. She tried to keep the dogs from being around the turtle a lot. She did not want Lulu trying to bite them or harm them. Her five friends did not want to give up on Lulu coming out of that shell or sticking her head out playing with them. The dogs were frisky all the time.

Lulu is Gone

Lulu lived with Miss Cathy and her five frisky friends for several months until one day in the summer she couldn't find her. Lulu was not hiding in the grass or under the trees. Lulu was no where to be found. She had brought Lulu another turtle that was found and she had vanished months earlier. Miss Cathy secured the fence after that. Today Miss Cathy does not know how Lulu escaped.

Miss Cathy hopes that Lulu went back into the wild safe and no harm or danger came to Lulu.

Ms. Cathy offered a reward for Lulu if anyone could find her. The neighbors looked and looked for Lulu and could not find her. The neighbors don't know what happened to Lulu as of today. Ms. Cathy bought a footstool in memorial of Lulu the friendly pet turtle. This footstool reminds her of how much she cared and loved Lulu the pet turtle. Miss Cathy and Lulu's five friends really miss her, even now.

I miss you, Lulu.

A Message From Cathy To Pet Lovers

Love Your Pets!!!

Do Some Researches About Animals

An estimated of 60 percent of households have or have had at least one pet. Do a research on "Can Pets Help You Live Longer! Berkeley University of California has a website. While you are sitting sometimes, just read it. A pet helps with a lot of loneliness in the home.

I am saying it again, "I love Scottie, Snowman, Princess, Peanut and Fluffy." I miss Lulu a lot because she allowed me to feed and care for her while we were together.

If you know of any pets being abused or treated with cruelty, please call The Humane's Society of the United States hotline or go to www.humane-society.org. You also can get in touch with the rspca.org.

Printed in the United States
By Bookmasters